Know
your
Fish

KNOW YOUR FISH

*An angler's guide to
British freshwater fish*

Leonard Brown

**COLOUR ILLUSTRATIONS
BY ERNEST PETTS**

ADAM & CHARLES BLACK
LONDON

FIRST PUBLISHED 1968
REPRINTED 1970, 1974
BY A. AND C. BLACK LIMITED
4, 5 AND 6 SOHO SQUARE LONDON W.1
TEXT © 1968 LEONARD BROWN
ILLUSTRATIONS © 1968 ERNEST PETTS

SBN 7136 0940 0

ACKNOWLEDGMENT

The colour plates in this book are reproduced
by kind permission of Brooke Bond Oxo Ltd.

Printed by The Berkshire Printing Co. Ltd., Reading.

CONTENTS

Going fishing for the first time, or any time for that matter, is an exciting business. But all too often a lot of the enjoyment is lost when the beginner somehow catches a fish but cannot identify it or when he knows what fish he is likely to catch but does not have that knowledge of the fish which will give him a greater chance of success.

To many people, one fish looks much the same as another and indeed there are fishes of different species which are extremely alike in their shape and colouring. In order to identify a fish with certainty it is necessary to study the parts of the fish:

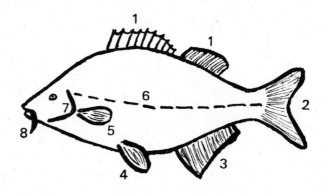

1. Dorsal fin   2. Tail fin   3. Anal fin   4. Pelvic fins
5. Pectoral fins   6. Lateral line   7. Gill cover   8. Barbel

The Body

Looked at from the side, freshwater fish may have a shape which varies between the symmetrical lines of, say, a torpedo to the shape of a dinner plate. Moreover, the plate-shaped fish may have a humped-back and a comparatively flat belly line, or vice versa. Fish are generally laterally compressed, that is, when viewed from the front it will be noticed that the height from belly to back is much greater than the width from side to side.

The colouring of any fish is extremely difficult to define, usually a mixture of subtle shades of brown, green, grey, bronze etc. In addition, fish of the same breed may differ according to their location, since the colour usually adapts to the surroundings to act as camouflage.

Even the food available and the chemical composition of the water in which the fish live may play a part in influencing colour.

The body is generally covered with scales, though the amount of scaling varies. A leather carp has none at all, the mirror carp has only patches of scales, while the mullet is scaled over the entire body and head. When trying to distinguish between two very similar types of fish it may be that the scales will give the answer. Although this answer may come from the shape and size it is better to identify by a scale count—probably along the lateral line. This line is present in all fish but may be hardly visible as in the shads, full length as in the pike, or only extending part of the way along the body as in the minnow.

All fish species differ, even if only slightly, in the position, shape and size of the fins. These are the tail or caudal fin, the dorsal fin or fins which are found on the back, the anal fin which is underneath and to the rear of the body, the two pelvic fins which are also underneath the body and either midway or to the rear, and the two pectoral fins which are found on either side of the body behind the gill-covers. All fresh-water fishes except the eel have two sets of paired fins. The dorsal and anal fins in particular are often used for identification, by counting the number of rays supporting the fin membrane. The rays may be spiny or soft. Some fish such as the salmon have a small adipose dorsal fin without rays.

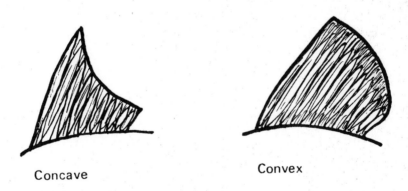

Concave   Convex

Two dorsal fin shapes

The Head

Although the general shape of the head may be a guide to identification, it may also be necessary to examine the mouth and the eyes. The mouth should be examined for shape (horizontal, downturned), size and position. These are often related to the habits of the fish—a bottom feeder will have the mouth set low or underneath the head, as in the gudgeon, while a surface feeding fish, such as the bleak, will have the mouth set high. This adaption to environment and habit will also be found in the eyes—set on each side of the head in fish which are nervous and preyed on by other fish, set high for surface feeders and set close together and forward to give binocular vision to hunting fish such as the pike. Note also the teeth or absence of teeth, and the thickness of lips.

SOME ANGLING TERMS EXPLAINED

Arlesey Bomb
A pear-shaped weight often used in leger fishing.

Bite Indicator
Bite indicators can be simple or complex, ranging from a piece of silver paper on the line to an electric buzzer. These indicators are generally used either for detecting very gentle bites or for night fishing. *See also* Swing-tip.

Breaking Strain
The strain necessary to break a dry line. The breaking strain will be less if the line becomes weakened through long usage, knots, etc., or when the line is wet.

Cast
A length of fine nylon (usually three or more feet) making up the final part of the line to the hook. Casts are mainly used in game fishing, and for wet fly fishing they may have additional, shorter lengths attached at intervals.

Casting
The art of presenting the bait on to the water.

Centre-pin Reel
A drum-type, free-running reel.

Dapping
A method of presentation by which a fly, often a live specimen is attached to the hook and allowed to 'dance' on the surface of the water above a fish's lie.

Dead-bait
A dead fish used as bait. Usually it is attached to a tackle which gives it apparent life and movement when drawn through the water.

Dry Fly

An artificial representation of a fly. The imitation may be very accurate of a particular kind of fly or one of the many patterns which have only a slight resemblance, if any, to a real fly.

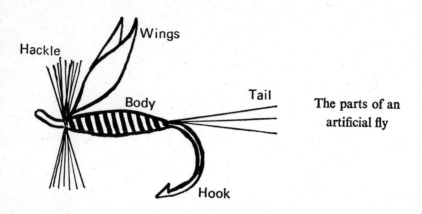

The parts of an artificial fly

Fixed-spool Reel

A reel with a stationary spool (at right angles to the rod direction) which, when the pick-up arm is down, allows the line to leave the spool freely without any movement of the parts of the reel. This practically eliminates reel over-run, the cause of many a tangle. When the winding arm is turned the pick-up arm is flicked back and begins to turn, taking up the line and re-winding it on to the spool.

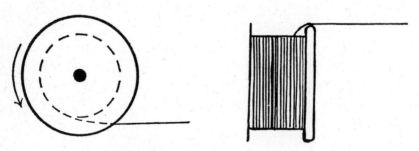

Line release principle of the centre-pin reel (left)
and the fixed-spool reel (right)

10

Floats

Floating objects designed to indicate bites and to hold terminal tackles at various levels in the water.

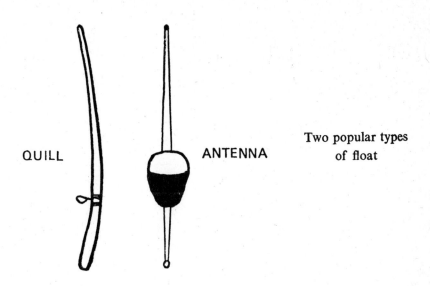

QUILL ANTENNA

Two popular types of float

Gaff

A long handled hook used for landing fish—generally heavy game fish such as salmon.

Groundbait

Food placed in the water to attract fish to the angler's swim.

Laying-on

Generally used in slow or still water. The bait rests on the bottom but without a lead as in legering and the float is adjusted to ride in a half-cocked position.

Leads

Lead weights used to sink baits below the water.

Legering

A form of fishing without a float—the line runs down to the bait through a sliding lead weight. The weight rests on the bottom and allows the line to run through it if the bait is taken. It can be prevented from sliding down on to the bait by split shot pinched on to the line.

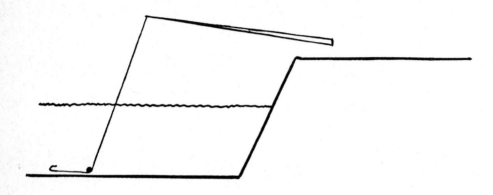

Leger tackle

Live-bait

A live fish used as bait.

Long Trotting

In this form of fishing the bait is allowed to move down stream with the current for quite long distances. It requires a delicate touch to keep the progress smooth and the float just behind the bait.

Maggots

Generally the larvae of the common bluebottle fly used as bait.

Multiplier Reel

A drum reel with a very free-running action and highly geared to retrieve line quickly. It is fixed above the rod, not below it as with fixed-spool and centre-pin reels.

Nets

Anglers nets are generally of two kinds—the keep-net, a tubular net closed at one end and semi-submerged to hold fish before they are released, and the landing-net, usually of a triangular shape and used for taking up fish as they are brought in on the hook.

Paternoster

Basically this form of tackle consists of two or three traces or spars projecting horizontally at different heights from a vertical line weighted to hold bottom. The hooks are attached to the ends of the horizontal traces.

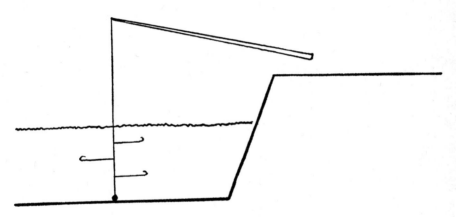

Paternoster tackle

Plugs

Plugs are imitations of small fish used as bait for pike and other predatory fish. They are constructed so as to wobble and move up and down in the water.

Prebaiting

Placing food in the water to attract fish to a particular swim some time before commencing to fish.

13

Priest

A metal club used for despatching fish by a blow on the head. They are generally only used for game fish since coarse fish should be returned to the water unharmed.

Rise

The action of a fish in coming to the surface to take food. It is also the term for the circular ripple made on the water by this action.

Sink and Draw

Usually used in dead-bait fishing for pike, perch etc. The bait is allowed to sink to the bottom, is then raised, allowed to sink, raised again, etc.

Snap-tackle

Terminal tackle used for holding a live-bait.

Split-shot

Small lead balls with slits in them so that they can be pinched on to the line.

Spoons

A lure consisting of a curved bar which revolves when drawn through the water giving the impression of a moving fish.

Strike

The act of raising the rod tip when a bite is felt to fix the hook firmly in the fish's mouth.

Swing-tip

A bite indicator consisting of an additional rod tip, hanging down so that it moves at the slightest movement of the bait.

Swivels

Swivels are devices for joining terminal tackles to the line so that the tackle can turn without twisting the line.

Tailer

A wire noose used for taking a hooked fish (generally a salmon) from the water. When pulled tight the noose grips the fish just in front of the tail.

Trotting
A method of fishing in which the float and bait are allowed to move for long distances down river.

Wet Fly
An artificial fly designed to float below the surface of the water. They are often fished in threes, the nearest fly being called the 'bob' fly, the intermediate one a 'dropper' and the end one the 'tail' fly.

Barbus barbus

Identification
The barbel has a rounded, smoothly tapering body. The colour of the back is a dark olive-green, the sides are a paler shade of green (often with a metallic sheen) and the belly is cream or white. Its thick-lipped mouth is set under the head and turned down at the corners with four barbels attached to it—two at the front of the upper lip and one at each corner. The brown-green dorsal fin is fairly short but the lower paired fins are relatively large for the size of the fish. The tail is deeply forked and has differently shaped lobes—the upper one being pointed and the lower rounded. The scales are quite small. There may be some difficulty in distinguishing the young barbel from a gudgeon, but the latter can usually be identified by its speckled fins. The average weight of an adult barbel would be 6 - 8lb.

Location
Barbel are found only in relatively few Southern and Eastern English rivers. They prefer swift, clear streams with clean, gravelly bottoms. Their favourite haunts are in the deep, fast currents close to weirs. Good barbel rivers are the Thames, Trent, Kennet, Dorset Stour and Hampshire Avon.

Feeding Habits and Baits
As might be guessed from its underslung mouth, the barbel is essentially a bottom feeder where it roots about for insect larvae, silkweed, shrimps and similar matter. It will also take minnows, frogs and worms in addition to the bread (flake, crust or paste), cheese, bunched maggots and artificial baits presented to it by the angler. Chopped worms or bread may be used as groundbait.

17

Fishing methods

A fairly powerful rod is necessary to control the terminal tackle in fast water and deal with the runs of a full-grown barbel. With this rod use a centre-pin or fixed-spool reel and 6 or 8 lb. b.s. line. The usual methods of fishing are legering or trotting down, although it has been known for a barbel to take a spinning lure.

Legering is generally used when only a limited length of bank is available. Use a sliding lead heavy enough to keep the tackle still on the bottom and stop it with a split shot about two feet from the hook, the line thus running virtually direct from the bait to the reel. An arlesey bomb type of weight may be used if a slowly moving bait is required.

If a reasonable length of bank is free then use a float and trot your bait downstream. Find the depth of the water and fix the float so that the hook gets down almost to the bottom. Let the tackle travel down for perhaps thirty or forty yards before bringing it back and starting again at a different distance from the bank. Make sure the bait is getting down near the bottom by putting split shot on the line and use a float that you can see at a distance. It is essential to keep the float behind the bait as it moves with the current.

Morone labrax

Identification
The body is long and tapers smoothly to the tail, rather resembling a salmon in shape. The blue-grey back with its metallic sheen has two dorsal fins, the one nearest the head being spiky or spiny and the rear one having softer, branched rays. These dorsal fins are a point of distinction between the bass and the salmon which has only one true dorsal fin, its second one being a small adipose projection with no spines or rays. The bass has a large mouth with sharp teeth, the gill covers are spiky and the cheeks are scaled. The average weight is in the 3 - 4 lb. range.

Location
Bass are to be found in the estuaries of Southern and Western England, Wales and Ireland. Although more common either in or near salt water, bass seem to have no particular dislike of fresh water and often find their way several miles upriver.

Feeding Habits and Baits
Good natural baits are crabs, prawns, ragworms, small fish and squid —one particular bait may be found to be particularly attractive to bass at a particular place and time for no obvious reasons. They may also take artificial baits such as spinning lures and artificial flies.

Fishing Methods
Tackle will vary according to the method being used. For example in legering a long-casting rod with a multiplying reel will give the best results using a two or three ounce fixed or sliding weight on 15-20 lb.

Continued on page 20

19

BASS
BLACK BASS

Micropterus salmoides

Identification
The large-mouthed black bass with its humped back rather resembles a perch but differs in having the rear dorsal fin with its branched rays higher than the forward, spiky, one. Its body shape is deep but narrow and there is an abrupt tapering towards the tail. In colour it is generally darker than the perch, having a dark olive-brown back with paler sides and a silvery-white belly. A dark horizontal stripe appears on each side. The mouth is large and down-turned with small bristly teeth. It has a rather small tail with hardly any fork. Not only the body but a large part of the head is scaled.

Location
This fish and the closely related small-mouthed black bass are uncommon in Britain and extremely localised having been introduced from America into various waters without much success.

Fishing Methods—continued
b.s. line. In very rough water it may be most profitable to use a paternoster style, otherwise a sliding weight may be used stopped at a swivel from which a trace of about three feet leads to the hook. Bass may also be taken by spinning with an artificial lure or live bait; or on a large wet or semi-wet fly.

Alburnus alburnus

Identification

The bleak has a slim laterally compressed body with a slightly curved back and a more strongly curved underside. It has an olive or grey-green back, silvery sides and belly and pale-coloured fins. The head is small with the mouth set high and turned down at the corners. The scales are very loosely attached to the body. Bleak rather resemble small dace from which they can be distinguished by the anal fin which is much longer in the bleak and has 15–20 rays as against 7–9 in the dace. They are usually 3 - 6 inches in length.

Location

Bleak are mainly found in the slow-flowing rivers of Midland, Eastern and Southern England (particularly the Thames), and occasionally in still water.

Feeding Habits and Baits

As can be expected from the high set of the mouth the bleak is generally a surface feeder (except in Winter) taking flies and tiny particles of food from, or just below, the surface. Good baits are single maggots, small pieces of bread or cheese and artificial flies.

Fishing Methods

The readiness of bleak to take a bait can be a nuisance to the angler who is after larger fish, but can provide a good deal of entertainment with the lightest of float tackle or with the artificial fly. It is essential to strike quickly when the bait is taken as the bleak make incredibly swift snatches at the bait. They may also, of course, be sought after as bait for the subsequent pursuit of pike or perch. Since bleak can be caught quickly and easily by the expert, they are quite popular with match fishermen.

21

BREAM
BRONZE BREAM

Abramis brama

Identification
The bronze bream is almost plate-shaped, having a very deep but narrow body (the depth may be as much as half the length) with a pronounced hump on the back. The fully grown fish has a dark greeny-brown or bronze back but when young has a mainly silvery colouring. The lower sides are a lighter shade of the back colour and the belly is creamy. It has a deeply forked tail with unsymmetrical lobes. The dorsal fin is quite short and on top of the hump, whilst the anal fin is relatively long for the size of the fish. The mouth is slightly down-turned and thick-lipped. Its body is covered in a thick layer of slime.

Location
Bream, usually in shoals, are common in slow-flowing waters of a reasonable depth in many parts of England but particularly in Central and Eastern districts, and in Ireland but not in Wales, Northern Scotland and Western England.

Feeding Habits and Baits
Bream are mainly bottom feeders, grubbing in the mud for worms, small aquatic creatures, vegetable matter etc. Good baits are worms, maggots and bread in flake, crust or paste form.

Fishing Methods
Bream tend to move about in shoals and it is therefore necessary to groundbait heavily as soon as one is caught. The equipment most generally used is a combination of Avon-type rod with a fixed spool reel and 3 lb. b.s. line. There are several methods of fishing but probably
Continued on opposite page

22

Blicca Bjoernka

Identification
The silver bream has a deep, flat body similar to but smaller than the bronze bream. The back is a dark olive-green, the sides a pale silver green and the belly white. The fins are pale and may be tinged with pink. With its general shape and similarities in the shape of the tail and other fins, silver bream of a reasonable size are often mistaken for young bronze bream and it may be necessary to make a scale and fin ray count to identify with certainty. Silver bream have 19–24 rays in the anal fin and 44–50 scales along the lateral line as against the bronze bream's 23–29 rays and 49–57 scales.

Location
Silver bream are less common than the bronze bream and tend to be found mainly in certain waters of Eastern England–South Yorkshire, Lincolnshire, Norfolk and Essex.

Feeding Habits and Baits
Like the bronze variety, silver bream feed on or near the bottom and will take worms, maggots and various bread baits.

Fishing Methods—continued
the most popular is legering in one form or another, mainly because it is suited to fishing in the deeper parts of both still and running water. Bream are shy takers and, when legering, some form of bite detector is most useful. Legering entails the use of a sliding weight which is stopped on the line a foot or so from the hook. Alternatively the laying-on method can be used in which a float is positioned on the line to allow the baited hook to lie on the bottom.

23

BULLHEAD

Cottus gobio

Identification
This rather ugly little fish, sometime's called "miller's thumb", has a large head and a flat, tadpole-shaped body. Its back is grey-brown with orange spotted paler sides and a creamy belly. It has no scales. The two dorsal fins are set close together and have serrated edges as have the large ruff-like pectoral fins and the anal fin. The tail is un-forked. The mouth is large and curves downward. Bullhead are usually 3 or 4 inches in length.

Location
The bullhead is common throughout England and Wales with a liking for shallow clear streams where it is often to be found hiding under stones and rocks.

Feeding Habits
Bullhead usually stay on the bottom of the stream swallowing any food particles, water creatures and fish small enough to enter its mouth.

Fishing Methods
These fish are not usually angled for except, possibly, for live bait as a last resort.

Lota lota

Identification
The burbot rather resembles a short and thickset eel but can be easily distinguished by the fact of its having two sets of paired fins. The back is a green-brown colour with darker blotches, the sides becoming lighter in colour and the belly cream. It has no scales. There are two dorsal fins, the first short and the second extremely long. The mouth is large with three barbels, one hanging from the lower jaw and two projecting upwards above the mouth.

Location
Burbot are quite rare except in the Eastern counties of England from Essex to Yorkshire. They like deep waters and the cover of weeds and stones, emerging at night to feed.

Feeding Habits and Baits
The burbot's diet is mixed, usually consisting of small fish, frogs and any small dead creatures in the water.

Fishing Methods
Because of their habit of feeding at night and their localised distribution burbot are not regularly sought by anglers.

CARP
COMMON CARP

Cyprinus carpio

Identification
The carp's body is thickset and deep. Its back is olive or bronze in colour becoming paler on the sides with a cream belly. The dorsal fin is long and concave. The mouth is thick-lipped and there are four barbels, two small ones at the middle of the upper lip and two large ones hanging from the corners of the mouth. Carp over 40lb are occasionally caught but most are in the 10 - 20lb class.

Location
Carp are to be found throughout Britain in lakes and ponds and occasionally in the quiet parts of slow-flowing rivers.

Feeding Habits and Baits
The natural food of the carp is the vegetable matter, weed, worms, insect larvae, crustaceans etc. which may be found on the lake bottom. Good artificial baits are bread crust, bunched worms or a partly boiled potato.

Fishing Methods
The rod for carp fishing should ideally be one designed for just this fish. With this rod a large capacity fixed spool reel and, say, 10 lb. b.s. line complete the basic outfit.
Carp fishing is best done late in the day or early in the morning during the summer months since the fish tend to feed only when the water temperature is at a certain level. Prebaiting for several days beforehand is well worth while. The standard method is to use neither float nor weight but to attach a large bait to a large hook and cast out to the desired spot. The rod is then put upon the rest pointing in the direction

Continued on opposite page

26

Carassius carassius

Identification
The crucian carp is generally much smaller than the common carp and may be immediately distinguished from it by its lack of barbels. Its body is relatively thicker and deeper than the common carp and, in fact, rather resembles a bream, but differs from it in its long dorsal and short anal fins. The back is usually a dark shade of olive-brown and the sides have a bronze colouration. The dorsal fin is generally convex which is another point of difference between it and the common carp. The average weight is about $1\frac{1}{2}$ lb.

Location
These fish are usually found in the lakes and ponds of Eastern and South Eastern England.

Feeding Habits and Baits
These are the same as for the common carp—vegetable matter, weed, worms, larvae, etc.

Fishing Methods—continued
of the bait, a bite indicator attached (a piece of silver paper on the line or a patent electric alarm) and the angler settles down to wait. The recovery arm of the reel is, of course, set to allow line to be taken freely. Another method is to stalk those carp which come near the bank to feed on the surface. It is usual to groundbait and, keeping out of sight of the fish, to have the hook bait poised just above the water level and ready to lower when a carp appears.

27

CARP
MIRROR CARP

Cyprinus carpio var

Identification
The mirror carp (and leather carp) are much the same in appearance and shape to the common carp, having four barbels and a long concave-edged dorsal fin. The mirror carp, however, is distinguished by its scales which are large, shiny and grouped in irregular patches over the body or perhaps in one or two rows along its sides. The leather carp has no scales.

Location
As with the common carp, mirror and leather carp are generally to be found in lakes and ponds throughout Great Britain.

Feeding Habits and Baits
The food of the mirror and leather carp is also the same as the common carp—vegetable matter, weed, worms, larvae, etc.

28

Silurus glanis

Identification
The catfish is rather like a gigantic, elongated tadpole with its wide, flat head tapering to a narrow tail. The colour of the back is a dark olive-brown, the sides are paler and mottled and the belly off-white. The mouth is extremely wide and armed with ferocious teeth. Four barbels hang from underneath the mouth and two extremely long ones trail from the upper lip. Its dorsal fin is small but the anal fin is long, running from about midway along the body almost to the tail. The tail fin is unforked.

Location
The Wels catfish has been introduced from Europe and is found only in some of the lakes and ponds of Bedfordshire and Buckinghamshire.

Feeding Habits and Baits
The catfish usually lurks in the mud or among thick weeds. It is a scavenger which will eat almost anything—fish, rats, frogs, vegetable matter, bread etc.

Fishing Methods
Catfish are not generally angled for.

CHAR

Salvelinus alpinus

Identification
The body shape of the char is very similar to that of its relation, the trout, including the small adipose fin on the back near to the tail. There are many varieties of char and therefore of colouring but generally the back is a dark blue-grey colour, the sides pale grey or silvery and the belly pink or yellow. There are many markings on the sides, usually orange or yellow spots. The average weight is about 1 lb.

Location
Char, generally, are deep-water fish and are found in occasional deep lakes throughout the British Isles, but particularly in the Lake District, Scotland, Ireland and Wales.

Fishing Methods
Because of the depths at which char are usually found they are not often angled for.

Squalius cephalus

Identification
The body is long and fairly round in section, particularly towards the head. The chub has a dark grey-green back with silvery-yellow sides and an off-white belly with occasionally a pinkish tinge to the head. The edges of the fins are rounded, the dorsal and tail fins being dark in colour with pinkish streaks and the lower fins are buff or pink; the tail may be edged with a darker colour. The large thick-lipped mouth is set well forward on the head and is downturned at the corners. Small chub have a silvery appearance and may resemble dace but can be distinguished by the fins which are convex in chub and concave in dace. An adult chub will probably weigh about 3 - 4 lb.

Location
The chub prefers running water with a hard bottom and has a liking for tree-lined banks from which a good deal of its food comes. Many older chub seem to establish themselves in a suitable bankside hole to which they return after feeding. They are quite common almost every-where in Britain except for Northern Scotland, Ireland, West Wales and Cornwall. Chub have lately become established in a small way in Ireland.

Feeding Habits and Baits
Chub tend to feed at all times of the day and in any weather and have a liking for insects, frogs, fruit, shellfish, worms etc. In addition to these items, wasp grubs, cheese, slugs, maggots, minnows and artificial flies and lures all make good baits.

31

Fishing Methods

The rod should be stout enough for use on a fast-running river with a centre-pin or fixed-spool reel and, say, 4 lb. b.s. line. One popular method is to trot the bait down to the fish from about twenty-five yards upstream, making sure that the line is well shotted near the hook to get the bait down quickly. Use a medium-sized float and control the line so that the float is always behind the bait. Check the line from time to time to make the bait rise and fall and vary the depth of the bait with each cast. A variation on this is to use a sliding weight stopped about a foot above the hook and a heavier float, the bait being allowed to roll along the bottom with the current.

Another widely used technique is legering which entails the use of a sliding lead (heavy enough to hold bottom) stopped a short distance from the hook. No float is used, the line running direct from rod to hook. A weight such as the arlesey bomb can be used to vary the style by moving the bait slowly along the bottom.

Fly fishing with a light trout rod can be most rewarding but it is also most difficult as the chub is an extremely shy fish and it is essential to approach quietly and stay hidden. A large fly or worm can be used. Chub will occasionally take a spinning lure or a live minnow. If it is possible to get very near to the fish and remain hidden a live fly or other insect may be attached to a small hook and allowed to dance or dap along the surface of the water just above the chub's lie.

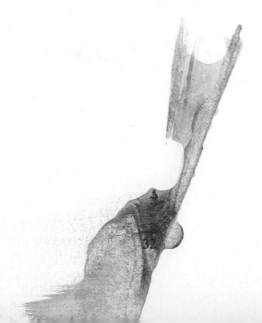

Leuciscus leuciscus

Identification
The dace has a slim tapering body with a dark olive or blue-green back and lighter coloured or silvery sides, the scales on which may have dark edges. The dorsal and anal fins have concave edges and, with the lower fins, are a pale grey shade sometimes tinged with pink. The mouth is small and turned down at the corners. Dace are sometimes confused with small chub but can be identified by their concave fins. There is also some similarity between dace and roach and in some cases it may be necessary to count the anal or dorsal fin rays. Dace have 7–9 and roach 9–12. The average weight is about ¾ lb.

Location
Dace are quite widespread in England and Wales (except the west) and are usually found in fast-flowing rivers.

Feeding Habits and Baits
All kinds of water insects, shellfish, larvae, flies etc., are eaten by dace. Good baits are bread crust and flake, maggots and, occasionally, silkweed. A brightly-coloured artificial fly may also prove successful.

Fishing Methods
Trotting with light tackle is an excellent method of fishing for dace. It may be necessary, however, to vary the depth of the bait from time to time. Alternatively the laying-on method may be used allowing the bait to lie on the bottom.
Dace may also rise freely to the fly and succumb to the wet-fly technique for trout. Three small flies should be mounted on a trace and cast across the stream, then drawn back as the current takes them down. It is essential to strike quickly.

EEL
YELLOW EEL

Anguilla anguilla

EEL
SILVER EEL

Anguilla anguilla

Identification

YELLOW EEL

The back is a dark brown colour, the sides being a paler shade and the belly yellow or cream. The body is snake-like with a long dorsal fin beginning a little way back from the head and extending to the tail. The anal fin starts further back and also extends to the tail.

SILVER EEL

The yellow eel, after leaving the Atlantic and entering our waters as an elver, stays for several years, before returning to the sea. When this is about to happen the eel's colouring begins to change. The back becomes dark, the belly silvery and a horizontal bronze stripe appears along the sides. Then, in the autumn, the silver eel (as it is now called) descends to the sea and crosses the Atlantic to spawn in the Sargasso Sea never to return.

Location
Born in the depths of the Atlantic, eels reach our rivers as small elvers and stay for several years of growth before returning to the sea. Eels are common everywhere in Britain even in some landlocked waters. They live in mud or in holes generally coming out to feed at night.

Feeding Habits and Baits
Eels feed on fish, frogs, insect larvae, worms, shellfish etc. Dead fish and large worms are the usual baits.

Fishing Methods
The catching of eels calls for crude equipment and even cruder methods. Use an old, strong rod and stout line. With a large bunch of worms or a dead fish as bait, cast out into a likely-looking spot—slow-flowing and deep water; if the eel takes the bait let the line run out for some distance before striking. It is then a matter of hauling him out by brute force and, more difficult, trying to despatch him, usually best done by severing the head.

FLOUNDER

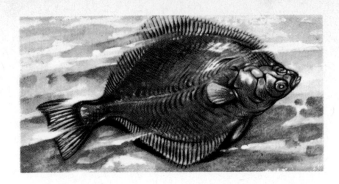

Platichthys flesus

Identification
The flounder has an extremely flattened shape. It is actually compressed sideways but early in its life one eye begins to move from one side to the other and the fish begins to swim on its side until it appears as though the fish is compressed from top to bottom. The mouth also becomes twisted towards the top. The back is usually a dark grey, olive or brown and covered with orange spots and blotches. The colour varies a great deal according to the colour of the river or sea bed on which the flounder is resting. The dorsal fin is almost always on the left side and extends almost from head to tail, the anal fin on the other side being only slightly shorter. The underside is a white or creamy colour. The weight is usually about 1 lb.

Location
Flounders can be found all round the coast of Britain in the estuaries of most unpolluted rivers.

Feeding Habits and Baits
All kinds of water creatures make good baits for flounder—ragworm, crab, shrimps, sand eels, etc.

Fishing Methods
There are various ways of fishing for flounder at sea but for inshore fishing a float tackle which allows the bait to just touch bottom should prove successful. It should not be necessary to use more than a single hook and here it should be remembered that flounder are shy in taking in food and it is necessary to strike late rather than early.

36

Thymallus thymallus

Identification
The grayling is a member of the salmon family as is shown by the adipose fin near its tail and it has the general shape of that family. Its back is a dark blue or olive colour and the sides are silvery with light grey horizontal lines, dark spots and a metallic purplish tinge. The dorsal fin is large for the size of the body with dark horizontal marks. The average weight is $1 - 1\frac{1}{2}$ lb.

Location
This fish likes clear, fast-flowing streams and is found mainly in the North of England and in Scotland. It has spread to the South of England and Wales but only to a few rivers and not in large numbers.

Feeding Habits and Baits
Grayling feed on flies, insect larvae, worms and small water creatures and will take both the game and coarse fisherman's baits—artificial flies, worms, maggots, etc.

Fishing Methods
Grayling fishing comes into its own during the Autumn and in the later months of the year. It has become traditionally the fish to which the trout fisherman turns when trout are no longer to be caught. Most of the fishing methods described under trout will catch grayling —dry fly, wet fly etc., but good sport can be had by fishing with roach tackle or with a fly rod and line to which is added a small float, the bait being worm or maggot. A small shot is fixed near the hook and the float positioned so that the bait just clears the bed of the stream. Using this tackle the bait should be allowed to be carried down by the current searching all likely lies.

37

GUDGEON

Gobio gobio

Identification
The gudgeon has a dark olive-brown back with paler flanks on which a row of darker blotches can generally be seen. The fins are usually a light grey in colour with darker markings. The large mouth is set low on the head and two barbels project from the corners. The scales are large for the size of the fish. Gudgeon are quite small, usually weighing only a few ounces.

Location
Gudgeon are very common in England except for Cornwall and the North West. They are less common in Ireland and not found at all in Scotland.

Feeding Habits and Baits
The diet of the gudgeon consists of such items as insects, larvae, worms, shellfish etc.

Fishing Methods
Because of their small size and the ease with which they can be caught if they are in a taking mood, gudgeon are not as popular with fishermen as many other fish although many anglers do set out to catch them for livebait. The finest of fine tackle should be used with just enough shot to cock a tiny quill float and the bait positioned so that it just touches the bottom without dragging. Raking the bottom a little way upstream often induces the gudgeon to start feeding.

*Coregonus
oxyrhynchus*

Identification
Houting are members of the group known as whitefishes which includes
the powan, pollan and vendace. The body is silvery and there is a small
adipose fin behind the dorsal fin and near to the tail. Its snout is
extremely pointed, with the mouth set back under the head.

Location
The houting is a sea fish found mainly in Northern waters but it is
occasionally found in some of our East Coast estuaries.

Fishing methods
Since houting only occasionally appear in British waters they are not
generally angled for, though they may very well take a bait intended for
a more common fish.

LOACH
SPINY LOACH

Cobitis taenia

Identification
The spiny loach has an elongated body only a few inches in length. Its back is a dark blue-green in colour, the sides being paler with darker blotches in a row along each side. Six short barbels of equal length, can be found around the mouth. The tail is not forked and has a rounded edge, as have the other fins. The spiny loach gets its name from the short spines set beneath the eyes. These spines can prove quite painful to the angler if the fish is handled carelessly.

Location
The spiny loach may be found in almost all parts of Great Britain except the most Northerly, usually in shallow, clear rivers and streams. It often advertises its presence by its habit of partly burying itself in sand which swirls up when it moves.

Feeding Habits
The loach feeds on minute water creatures and particles of vegetable matter.

Fishing Methods
Loach are not usually angled for, except perhaps as aquarium specimens or as bait.

LOACH
STONE LOACH

Cobitis barbatula

Identification
The stone loach, slightly larger than the spiny variety, has a slender body. Its colouring is a dark blue-green with paler sides on which are light and dark blotches. There are six barbels attached to the mouth—two short ones at the centre of the upper lip, a pair of larger ones at the centre of the lower lip and another pair at the corners of the mouth. The fins have rounded edges and are often dotted or striped. The tail has a very slight fork.

Location
Stone loach may be found in almost all parts of Great Britain except the most Northerly, usually in clear, shallow rivers and streams. As may be guessed from their name they usually can be found beneath stones on the bed of the stream.

Feeding Habits
The loach feeds on minute water creatures and particles of vegetable matter.

Fishing Methods
Loach are not usually angled for, except perhaps as aquarium specimens or as bait.

41

MINNOW

Phoxinus phoxinus

Identification
The minnow is a tiny fish being only an inch or so in length but with a perfectly developed fish-like shape. The back is usually a shade of dark green or brown though the colouring varies a good deal. The sides are a paler shade dappled with darker markings. The belly is usually white but in Spring the male's is bright pink. The fins have rounded edges except for the tail which is slightly forked.

Location
These fish are found everywhere in Great Britain except the most Northerly parts, and like clear water with a gravelly bottom. They are usually found in large shoals.

Feeding Habits
Minnows feed on minute water creatures and vegetable matter.

Fishing Methods
Minnow are not usually angled for except as aquarium specimens or as bait.

MULLET
GREY MULLET

Mugil chelo—
thick-lipped
Mugil capito—
thin-lipped

Identification
Both these species have broad heads with small mouths having either thick or thin lips. The back is a metallic blue colour and the sides are silvery with many horizontal grey stripes. There are two dorsal fins, those on the thin-lipped being smaller and farther apart than on the thick-lipped. The body is almost entirely covered in scales which extend very nearly to the front of the head.

Location
Both species are found in the estuaries of South and South West England though the thick-lipped is the more widespread and has even been caught in the estuaries of Southern Ireland.

Feeding Habits and Baits
Mullet feed on small water creatures and soft vegetable matter. They are quite indiscriminate feeders and all kinds of baits may be effective, providing they are soft in texture—bread paste, cheese, worms etc.

Fishing Methods
Groundbaiting is important and light tackle is essential. Because of the soft and sensitive mouth it is necessary to strike rather late and to play the fish gently.

PERCH

Perca fluviatilis

Identification
The perch has a hump-backed body with an olive-green back, paler green or yellow sides, and a white belly. There are several dark vertical stripes along the sides. Of the two dorsal fins, the forward one is large and spiky with a dark spot at the rear; the second dorsal is made up of soft branched rays. The lower fins are usually tinged with pink and the tail, which is relatively small, may also have pink markings. The gill covers are pointed and may bear small spikes. The mouth is large and downturned and the lips are rather soft and easily torn on the hook. The average weight is about 1 lb.

Location
Perch are quite widespread throughout the British Isles except for Scotland and may be found in still and running water.

Feeding Habits and Baits
Although the perch feeds mainly on small fish of all kinds it will also eat insects, shellfish, worms etc. All kinds of baits will be taken by perch—live or dead fish, worms, maggots, frogs and so on.

Fishing Methods
Most forms of angling can be used on perch. One of the more popular is float fishing particularly with a live bait such as a lip-hooked minnow. With this tackle the water should be searched from mid-water to the river bed. Deep swims are probably better fished with leger tackle, that is, with no float and with a sliding weight stopped a little way from the hook. A variation of this is the paternoster tackle with a stand-off trace tied about a foot above the weight. Spinning is also popular using a natural bait or an artificial lure, and can be varied by using a 'sink and draw' technique with a dead bait. There are times in late summer also when perch can be taken on a wet fly.

Esox lucius

Identification

The pike has a long tapering body with the anal and dorsal fins set well back towards the tail. The colouring has a marbled effect in green and yellow, darker on the back than on the sides. The fins have rounded edges and are green with brown markings. The head is large (rather like a duck's bill) with a projecting lower jaw and extremely sharp teeth. Size varies a good deal but 10 - 15 pounders are not uncommon.

Location

Pike are found everywhere in the British Isles particularly in waters with plenty of weed cover.

Feeding Habits and Baits

Pike will take almost any moving object — fish, frogs, waterbirds, rats, worms etc. Baits vary from live and dead fish to artificial spoons and lures.

Fishing Methods

Special rods have been developed for pike fishing with live and dead-baits, but if using a non-specialist rod, make sure it is strong enough to cast a heavy bait. A wire trace to the hook is essential in view of the pike's sharp teeth. A lighter rod and line can be used for spinning.

A study of the water is never wasted when in pursuit of pike. In lakes and rivers it will often be found that certain spots seem to attract them. They may also be seen in the water if the angler is unobtrusive and if a live or dead bait can be put in their path a catch is quite likely. This study and stalking of pike is much more effective than throwing the bait in anywhere and hoping that the pike will find it.

When spinning, the golden rule is to fish deep and slow. Although the pace may be varied occasionally, never let the bait stop altogether and keep it in the water to the last moment.

45

PIKE PERCH

Lucioperca lucioperca

Identification
The Pike perch is not a hybrid as its name suggests but a separate species. Its body is long and tapering with two long dorsal fins. Of these fins the first is spikey like that of the perch, but without a black spot, and the second fin is similar in size to the first but has softer spines. The back is a dark grey-green colour shading to paler sides on which can be seen broad vertical stripes of a darker shade. Like the pike it has a large mouth and many sharp teeth.

Location
Pike perch, which are common in Central Europe have been introduced to a few waters in England, notably Claydon Lake in Buckinghamshire and the Great Ouse.

Feeding Habits and Baits
Like the perch, the pike perch feeds on small fish, insects, worms etc. Baits used are generally live-bait or spinning lures.

Fishing Methods
As pike perch are introduced into new waters, their popularity will certainly grow. They are extremely good fighters and can be fished for with much the same tackle and methods as for the perch though it will be found necessary to use a wire trace to the hook. A lip-hooked live bait can be fished with a float, leger style, or on paternoster tackle. Pike perch will also pursue and take all kinds of spinning lures, plugs and spoons and occasionally an artificial fly.

*Coregonus clupeoides
spp*

Identification
The powan group of white fishes have slim, smoothly tapering bodies with dark blue-green backs and silvery sides. There is a small adipose fin between the dorsal fin and the tail. The average weight is about 1 - 2 lb.

Location
The powan is confined to the Loch Lomond district of Scotland but closely related fish called skelly and gwyniad may be found in the Lake District and Wales respectively.

Fishing Methods
Fish of the Powan group inhabit only a few deep lakes and lochs and are rarely caught by the angler.

ROACH

Rutilus rutilus

Identification

The colour of the roach varies a good deal but generally the back is dark green, blue, brown or almost black. The sides are silvery or brassy and the belly white. The dorsal and tail fins are generally darker than the lower fins and may be tinged with pink, especially the anal fin. The dorsal fin is concave and begins directly above the base of the ventral fins. The anal fin is also concave and is quite short. The mouth is quite small with a projecting upper lip. Identification may be made more difficult by the presence of roach-bream hybrids which may be distinguished with some certainty by counting the rays in the anal fin. If there are fifteen or more the fish is a hybrid, if twelve or less, a roach. The average weight is about 1 lb.

Location

Roach are found in most waters of Great Britain except for Northern Scotland. They prefer rivers with a steady flow, a hard bottom and good weed growth.

Feeding Habits and Baits

Roach feed generally on small water creatures, snails, insects, silkweed etc. Good baits are maggots, worms, grubs, wheat, bread, silkweed, hempseed etc.

Fishing Methods

Trotting, a popular method for roach, entails finding the depth of the stream to fix the distance between hook and float, and shotting the cast about a foot above the hook sufficiently to cock a small quill float. The bait is cast out and carried downstream just above the bottom for about twenty or thirty yards before retrieving and beginning again. It is essential to hold back the float occasionally so that the bait is always ahead of it but not so much that it causes the bait to rise in the water. It may pay occasionally to vary the depth of the bait since roach do sometimes change from bottom feeding, and indeed will, on occasion, succumb to the artificial fly, usually the sunken wet fly. Another useful method, especially for late season fishing, is legering. Here the float is dispensed with and a running weight is slipped down the line stopped by a split shot nipped on about a yard from the hook.

RUDD

*Scardinius
erythrophthalmus*

Identification

The rudd has a rather narrow but deep body and a slightly humped back. Its colour varies a good deal from one location to another but the back is generally a shade of green-brown and the silvery sides have a golden tinge which becomes more pronounced as the fish ages. The belly is a creamy white. The fins and sometimes the lips are pink or even red, the tail sometimes showing darker streaks. The mouth is down-turned with a projecting lower lip. The dorsal fin is set rather far back on the body. Confusion in identification may arise from the presence of bream-rudd hybrids which will be found to have fifteen to eighteen anal fin rays while the rudd will have ten to thirteen. There is also some similarity with the roach (in Ireland rudd have usually been called roach) but differences may be seen in the deeper body of the rudd and also in the mouth, the roach's being small and almost horizontal and the rudd's downturned with a larger lower jaw. The dorsal fin in relation to the ventral fins, is set further forward on the roach than the rudd. The average weight is about 2 lb.

Location

The rudd is quite widespread in England (particularly Norfolk), Wales and Ireland, being found in ponds and lakes and slow-flowing rivers.

Feeding Habits and Baits

Rudd feed in the upper part of the water as well as on the bottom on a variety of items such as insects, shellfish, worms and vegetable matter.

Fishing Methods

Generally the methods used for roach will be successful but an even lighter tackle should be used. Rudd take the artificial fly freely during the summer months, especially if a maggot is added to the fly hook.

Acerina cernua

Identification
This small fish is a relative of the perch. Its body is olive-grey or brown, covered with many darker spots. It has two dorsal fins, the first being spiny and the second, which is joined to it, made up of soft rays. The leading edges of the lower fins are spiny and the gill covers have sharp edges. The fins generally are a pale olive in colour and are speckled, as is the tail. The mouth is small with bristly teeth. Ruff rarely exceed about 4 inches in length.

Location
Ruff are common in Central and Eastern England, being found usually in lakes and the quieter parts of rivers.

Feeding Habits and Baits
The ruff is mainly a bottom feeder on vegetable matter and small aquatic creatures.

Fishing Methods
Ruff are not usually fished for, though they may take a bait meant for some other fish.

SALMON

Salmo salar

Identification
The back of the adult salmon is a dark, blue-black colour with a pronounced metallic sheen. The sides are silvery with dark spots and the belly is white. There are two dorsal fins, although the rear one is unlike a normal fin being an adipose projection without rays or spikes. Young salmon have distinctive markings—in the 'parr' stage (the first two years as a recognizable fish) it has a series of dark oval markings along each side and these become covered with a silvery coat as it becomes a 'smolt' and travels down to the sea. On its return from the sea as a 'grilse' it has the appearance of the adult salmon described above. After spawning, the salmon, now known as a 'kelt', attempts to return to the sea and at this stage is in poor condition with dull scales and a lean appearance. Size varies a great deal and salmon of anything between ten and thirty pounds may be taken.

Location
Salmon may be found in many parts of Great Britain where there are unpolluted rivers running to the sea. Scotland, Ireland, Wales and some parts of Western England are noted for their salmon fishing.

Feeding Habits and Baits
Strictly speaking, the salmon does not feed after returning to the river to spawn. However, it does take the artificial fly, spinning lure or natural baits such as the prawn when they are offered but it is not known whether this is the result of annoyance at their presence, a reflex action on seeing food, or hunger.

Fishing Methods
Fly
Since the salmon to all intents and purposes does not feed while in our rivers, it has always been a mystery why they will take a fly at all; there is no doubt that certain salmon fly patterns have proved more successful than others but even these successful ones hardly resemble any of the usual creatures to be found in a river. Perhaps it is simply annoyance at the presence of something alien that causes a salmon to snap at the fly. Except that the rod is generally longer and stouter and the tackle heavier, the technique is very similar to dry fly fishing for trout though it is necessary, to a certain extent, to search the water rather than to try and spot a particular fish.

Spinning
Spinning for salmon becomes more popular every year. On rivers, except where the water is high and running fast, the tendency is to use light, almost trout-weight, tackle with natural or artificial baits, spoons, lures etc. Casting is usually done across or upstream to bring the bait down and towards the caster. The bait should be kept quite close to the river bed. On lakes and locks spinning is generally done from a boat, either by casting from a drifting boat or trolling or towing the spinning bait from a rowed boat.

SHAD
ALLIS SHAD

Alosa alosa

SHAD
TWAITE SHAD

Alosa finta

Identification
The Allis Shad has a deep but narrow body with a row of scales along its underside giving a serrated effect. In colour the back is a blue-green or olive green with paler sides. The twaite shad is similar to but smaller than the allis shad and has a row of dark blotches on the upper flanks. The lateral line, although, of course, present, is not visible in either of the shads.

Location
The number of estuaries which the allis and twaite shad can use for the spawning run is being reduced every year by pollution and their presence is now extremely localised, mainly on the South West coasts of Britain.

Fishing Methods
Due to the spread of pollution, shad are confined to a few clean rivers and although they are netted they are not generally angled for.

Osmerus eperlanus

Identification
The small adipose fin near the tail shows the smelt to be a relation of the salmon. The body is slim with a very narrow taper at the tail. The body is blue-green with silvery sides on which can be seen short lateral lines at the gill covers. The tail has a pronounced fork and the fins have rounded edges. The mouth is large with relatively large teeth. The average weight is about $\frac{1}{2}$ lb.

Location
Pollution of estuaries has diminished the location of the smelt until they are now to be found only in some of the rivers on the Western Coast of Britain.

Feeding Habits and Baits
Smelt feed on small fish and water creatures.

Fishing Methods
Smelt are quite often taken by the angler as they travel up river to spawn, but because of their restricted location, they are not generally angled for.

STICKLEBACK

Three-Spined
Stickleback

*Gasterosteus
aculeatus*

STICKLEBACK

Ten-Spined
Stickleback

Pygosteus pungitius

Identification

The three-spined variety of stickleback is larger than the ten-spined, being generally 3–4 ins. in length and has a slim rounded body becoming very slender at the tail. The back is a blue-green colour with silvery sides often having speckles of blue and pink. In Spring the males become brightly coloured with a red belly and dark markings on the sides and back. There are three strong spines on the back with a soft dorsal fin behind them quite near to the tail which is unforked.

The ten-spined stickleback has a slim tapering body. Its colouring is olive or blue-green on the back with silvery sides and belly. In Spring the male's colouring becomes darker. It has 9–11 short spines along its back, projecting alternately left and right. The tail is unforked.

Location

Stickleback may be found in most parts of Great Britain except the most Northerly. It is the curious habit of the male to build a nest in which the fertilized eggs are kept during the breeding season.

Acipenser sturio

Identification
The sturgeon has a long tapering body coming almost to a point at the head. Around the body and extending along it are five rows of bony shields or studs. The mouth is set well back underneath the head, with four barbels hanging down nearer the snout. The fins, except for the pelvic, are set close to the tail, the upper lobe of which is much larger than the lower. The body is scaleless but with a strong, rough-textured skin. In colour the back is grey or brown with paler sides and creamy belly.

Location
Although quite common in some European rivers the sturgeon is only occasionally found in British estuarial waters.

Fishing Methods
Because of its rarity the sturgeon is not seriously angled for although occasionally caught on rod and line when other fish are being sought.

TENCH

Tinca Tinca

Identification
The tench has a short, thickset body, the colour varying from olive to dark brown. The sides are a lighter shade and the fins are dark and have rounded edges. The tail is relatively large and is almost unforked. There are two small barbels at each side of the mouth which is small and downturned with thick leathery lips. Other distinguishing features are the small, red eyes, the long lateral lines, the small scales and the coating of slime on the body. The usual weight is about 1 lb.

Location
Tench are to be found in most areas of the British Isles except for Northern Scotland. Their preference is for ponds and lakes but are also to be found in slow-flowing rivers with plenty of weed cover.

Feeding Habits and Baits
Tench usually feed at night, foraging in the mud for worms, snails, vegetable matter etc. Bread, maggot and worm have proved good baits.

Fishing Methods
June to August are usually reckoned to be the best months for tench fishing and best results will often be had by fishing early or late in the day when the sun is off the water. A clear patch on the bottom but with some nearby weed growth is a likely spot for tench and should be pre-baited if possible. In good conditions use a small float and adjust the position to get the hook bait just touching bottom. Alternatively, and particularly in unsettled weather, a running leger style may be used—discard the float and put a sliding weight on the line stopped by a split shot about eighteen inches from the hook. Tench are not bold takers and it may be necessary to use a bite indicator.

58

TEA TOWELS

In a high-quality fabric

Made with pure cotton for exceptional absorbency

With sturdy, incorporated hanging loop and intricate embroidery

Size: 50 x 70 cm

2-pack

Material: 100% cotton

Suitable for tumble dryers

VISKESTYKKER

I en god kvalitet

Særlig god sugeevne pga. ren bomuld

Med en robust, indarbejdet strop og flot broderi

Mål: 50 x 70 cm

2 stk.

Materiale: 100% bomuld

Tåler tørretumbler

Kvalitetsstempel
Testet for: Skadelige stoffer, Forarbejdning

QUALITY LABEL
Tested for:
✓ Hazardous substances
✓ Workmanship
c-mark ID:DEC-09-000-075

BUREAU
VERITAS

Slimsberasnobra V
D-74172 Neckarsulm

BROWN TROUT.

BROWN TROUT

Salmo trutta

TROUT PARR

Identification

The colouring and marking of trout vary a great deal from district to district. However, the back is usually a dark brown or olive colour and the sides may be silvery, brown or pink with darker spots and rings. The body is round in section tapering smoothly to the tail which is unforked. There is a small adipose fin between the dorsal fin and the tail. In the first stage of its life as a recognisable fish the trout (like the salmon and sea trout) is called a 'parr'. It is then about three inches long and has a row of dark spots along its sides. The adult trout size varies according to location from $\frac{1}{2}$ lb to 2 lb and over.

Location

Brown trout are to be found in most parts of the British Isles where clean, unpolluted water is to be found.

Feeding Habits and Baits

Trout feed on insects and larvae, shellfish, worms and small fish. The classic bait is the artificial fly but other baits are worms, live and dead fish, natural flies and artificial spinning lures.

Fishing Methods

Wet Fly Fishing—this method is traditionally practised on fast-flowing streams in Wales, the North of England and Scotland. In this style the artificial fly is allowed to sink under the surface of the water though usually not to any great depth. The casting of the fly is a complex business and cannot be fully dealt with in a book though there are some points which must be remembered at all times. It is essential that the recovery of the line from the water and the forward cast have separate paths; the line on the back cast must be allowed to extend fully and the rod must be checked on the forward cast so that the fly and line settles gently on to the water. Any number of flies may be tied on to the cast though three are generally used for normal wet-fly fishing reducing to one if the stream abounds with snags. The simplest method is to cast the flies on to the stream and allow the current to take them downstream It may, however, be more profitable (though more difficult) to cast upstream and let the flies come back to the rod. The moment at which the fish takes the fly cannot usually be seen with this method but should be felt as the bite is usually enthusiastic. Lake fishing is generally done from a boat since the area that can be covered from the bank is relatively limited. If fishing from the bank, however, it should be remembered that more and better sport is likely if casting is done from the bank on to which the wind is blowing since that is where the food and therefore the fish will be.

Dry Fly Fishing—whereas the wet fly fisherman fishes the water where he hopes the fish will be, the dry-fly man fishes the rise, that is he looks for the presence of a trout and casts one fly on to the water so that it will float on the surface over the fish. Traditionally, this form of fishing was practised on the slow-flowing chalk streams of the South of England. In recent years, however, anglers have had good results with the dry fly on what look like wet-fly rivers. The rise for which the dry-fly man looks is often dependent on the hatch of various natural flies and for this reason a good deal of attention is paid to the idea of making up an exact imitation of whatever fly is on the water. The use of exact imitations of natural flies is a controversial subject, however, and most trout fishermen have their own theory as to what really attracts the trout.

Worm Fishing and Dapping—worm fishing for trout can be extremely effective if not quite so satisfying as fly fishing. In dark, flood water it can be simply a matter of lowering a worm into a likely bankside spot where the water is comparatively calm and waiting for the trout to smell it out. However, the worm can also be used in place of a fly, fishing it upstream and allowing it to roll back with the current towards the rod. The form of fishing known as dapping entails the use of a live insect, perhaps a bluebottle, a mayfly or a daddy longlegs, placed on the hook and allowed to dance along the surface of the water. This necessitates a stealthy approach to the bankside and as little disturbance as possible both in noise and movement.

Spinning—on many waters spinning is not allowed but there are places where it can be practised and it is occasionally permitted on 'fly only' waters when conditions do not permit fly fishing.

TROUT
BROOK TROUT

Salvelinus fontinalis

Identification and Location
In shape the brook trout is similar to the brown trout but differs in colouring particularly on the dorsal fin and the tail, the brook trout's having dark horizontal stripes of colour on the dorsal and vertical stripes on the tail. The back is dark brown or olive with paler sides having a pinkish tinge and a pattern of dark spots.

The brook trout was introduced from America but has not become at all widespread. It can be found in a few deep lakes in North Wales and the Lake District.

TROUT
RAINBOW TROUT

Salmo irideus

Identification and Location
In its shape and general colouring the rainbow is very similar to the brown trout but can be easily identified by the red speckling or rainbow band on its sides and the dark spots on the tail which is slightly forked. Rainbow trout were introduced from North America into many rivers and lakes of Great Britain with varying degrees of success. They have disappeared from many waters though they have generally done better in lakes than in rivers.

62

TROUT
SEA TROUT

Salmo trutta

SEA TROUT PARR

Salmo trutta

Identification

The sea trout is the migratory form of brown trout. The brown trout itself is subject to variations in colour but generally the sea trout is larger and rather silvery. It is usually easier to identify it because of where it is caught than by differences in appearance. Sea trout, however, can be very similar to salmon and it may be necessary to make a fin-ray or scale count, e.g. counting the scales down from the rear of the adipose fin to the lateral line a salmon will have 10–13 and a sea trout 13–16. Like the salmon, the sea trout goes through the 'smolt' stage when, after two or three years in fresh water, it goes down to the sea. Sea trout smolt very often have orange coloured fins while the salmon has pale-coloured fins except the pectoral fins which are dark.

Location
Sea trout are almost invariably found in the rivers of the West Coast of Britain.

Fishing Methods
Sea trout are essentially a summer fish and June is considered a good month though there are of course 'early' and 'late' rivers. Generally the methods used are the same as for the brown trout, but the best fishing for sea trout is almost always to be had at night.